Put Beginning Readers on the Right Track with
ALL ABOARD READING™

The All Aboard Reading series is especially for beginning readers. Written by noted authors and illustrated in full color, these are books that children really and truly *want* to read—books to excite their imagination, tickle their funny bone, expand their interests, and support their feelings. With four different reading levels, All Aboard Reading lets you choose which books are most appropriate for your children and their growing abilities.

Picture Readers—for Ages 3 to 5
Picture Readers have super-simple texts with many nouns appearing as rebus pictures. At the end of each book are 24 flash cards—on one side is the rebus picture; on the other side is the written-out word.

Level 1—for Preschool through First Grade Children
Level 1 books have very few lines per page, very large type, easy words, lots of repetition, and pictures with visual "cues" to help children figure out the words on the page.

Level 2—for First Grade to Third Grade Children
Level 2 books are printed in slightly smaller type than Level 1 books. The stories are more complex, but there is still lots of repetition in the text and many pictures. The sentences are quite simple and are broken up into short lines to make reading easier.

Level 3—for Second Grade through Third Grade Children
Level 3 books have considerably longer texts, use harder words and more complicated sentences.

All Aboard for happy reading!

Special thanks to Bruce Rideout, Department of Psychology, Ursinus College.

Library of Congress Cataloging-in-Publication Data

Cole, Joanna.
    You can't smell a flower with your ear / by Joanna Cole ; illustrated by Mavis Smith.
       p.   cm. — (All aboard reading)
    1. Senses and sensation—Juvenile literature. [1. Senses and sensation.]
I. Smith, Mavis, ill. II. Title. III. Series.
QP434.C63 1994
612.8'5—dc20   93-27264
                                                  CIP
ISBN 0-448-40470-2 (GB)   A B C D E F G H I J   AC

ISBN 0-448-40469-9 (pbk.)   E F G H I J

ALL
ABOARD
READING™

**Level 2
Grades 1-3**

You Can't Smell a Flower with Your EAR!

All About Your 5 Senses

By Joanna Cole

Illustrated by
Mavis Smith

Grosset & Dunlap • New York

It's your birthday!

There's a surprise for you.

Your mom puts a blindfold on you.

A moment later you smell chocolate.

Then something is put in your mouth.

You taste sweet cake.

"But that is not the real surprise,"
says your sister.

"Put out your hand," says your dad.

You touch something soft.

You hear a little mew!

Before you pull off the blindfold,

you know what you will see.

It's a kitten!

6

Every day you use
your nose to smell,

your tongue to taste,

your skin to feel,

your ears to hear,

and your eyes to see!

These are your five sense organs.

Each one tells you something different

about the world around you.

They do this by sending

messages to your brain.

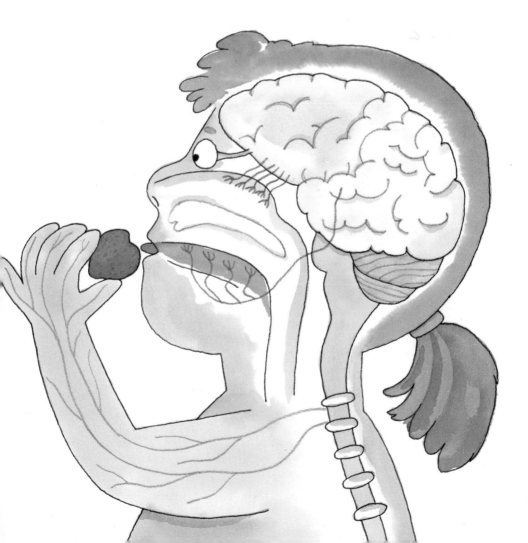

SEEING

Is your eyeball really a ball?

Yes!

Most of your eye is hidden

inside your skull.

Here is what your whole eye looks like.

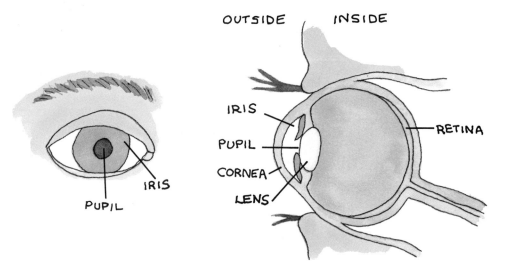

FRONT VIEW   SIDE VIEW

Each of your eyes has an opening

to let in light.

That opening is called the pupil.

Try This

Dim the lights.

Look at your eyes in a mirror.

Are your pupils big?

Now turn on a bright light.

Did you see your pupils get smaller?

Your pupils get bigger and smaller

to let in just the right amount of light.

Your eyes are made to see.

How do they work?

Look at a hat.

Light bounces off the hat

and goes into your eye.

The light hits the back of your eyeball.

A picture of the hat is made there.

Nerves—like wires—

carry messages about the picture

from the back of your eye

to special places in your brain.

You need your brain <u>and</u> your eyes

to see.

Sometimes your eyes see things

that don't make sense.

Then your brain tries

to make sense of them.

Try This

You see a'friend

coming down the street.

While he is still far away,

hold up your thumb.

Your eyes say that he looks

<u>smaller</u> than your thumb!

But your brain is not fooled.

Your friend only looks small

because he is far away.

You know that he is still big.

Sometimes you <u>can</u> fool your brain.

Try This

Look at the picture.

Which tree is bigger?

Did you say the red one?

No! Both are the same size.

Measure them and see.

Why does the red tree seem bigger?

Because the artist drew the picture

with lines that make the red tree seem

farther away.

Your brain acts the way it did

when you saw your friend

down the street.

It tells you the red tree is bigger

than it really is.

Sometimes you can see

two pictures in one.

Try This

In this picture,

do you see a white vase?

Or do you see two black dogs

looking at each other?

You may see one picture,

and then the other.

But your brain cannot see

both pictures at once.

HEARING

You want to fool your friend.

You say, "You can't see your ears."

"Yes, I can," says your friend.

Who is right? You both are!

Your friend can see

the outside part of her ears.

But she cannot see the other parts.

Those are inside her head.

The inside parts are the true,

hearing parts of the ear.

Your ears pick up

sound waves in the air.

Sound waves are tiny movements

or vibrations.

(You say it like this: vie-BRAY-shuns.)

You can hear vibrations.

Sound vibrations in the air go
into your ear.
They hit a stretchy skin—
your eardrum.
Then the eardrum vibrates, too.
On the other side of the eardrum
are three tiny, tiny bones.
These bones start to vibrate, too.

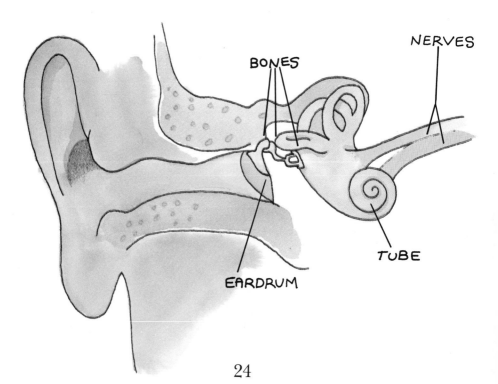

Beyond the bones is a tube
filled with liquid.
The liquid starts to vibrate, too.
These vibrations make
nerves near the tube
send messages
to your brain's hearing centers.
You need your ears
<u>and</u> your brain to hear.

Some animals have big outside ears
shaped like funnels.
Their ears can catch more sound waves
than your flat ears can.
You can find out what it's like
to have big outside ears.

Try This

Turn on a radio or TV.

Play it very softly.

Stand on the other side of the room.

Cup your hands behind your ears.

The sound seems louder, doesn't it?

Your ears also tell your brain
where a sound is.

Try This

Tell a friend to hide.

You cannot see her.

But if she makes a noise,

you know where to look.

That is because the sound

reaches one ear first.

Then it reaches your other ear.

The difference is very, very small.

But your brain can tell.

PSST...

SMELLING

You are walking past a pizza place.

There is a hot pizza in the oven.

You cannot see the pizza.

But your nose tells you it is there!

That's because your

nose is made

for smelling.

How does your nose smell?

When the pizza is baking,

tiny bits go out of the oven.

These bits are called molecules.

(You say it like this: MOLL-uh-kewls.)

Molecules are so small

we cannot see them.

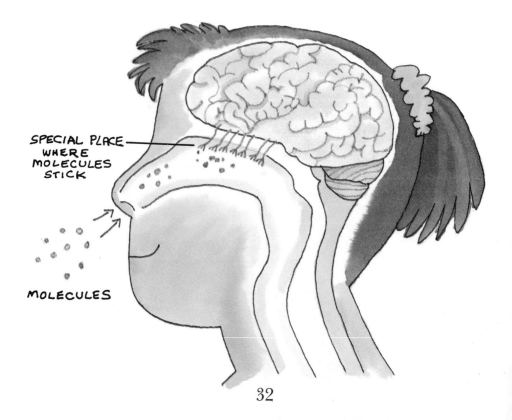

SPECIAL PLACE
WHERE
MOLECULES
STICK

MOLECULES

When you breathe in air,

pizza molecules go into your nose.

High up in your nose

is a special place

where molecules can stick.

Nearby nerves send messages

about the pizza molecules

to your brain.

Then you smell the pizza.

Try This

Find something that smells good—

flowers, soap, apples, or oranges.

Go near and breathe

the way you usually do.

Do you smell the nice smell?

Now put your nose near and <u>sniff</u>.

The smell is stronger now.

Why?

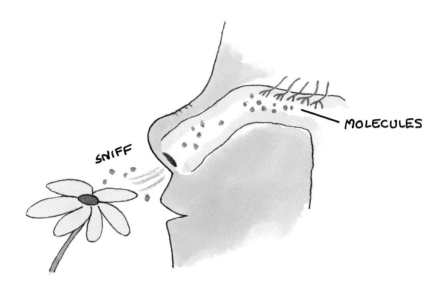

SNIFF

MOLECULES

When you sniff, you pull air
straight up your nose.
More molecules stick near the nerves,
so you get more of the smell.

TASTING

That pizza <u>smells</u> so good,

it must <u>taste</u> great, too.

Thank goodness you have taste buds

on your tongue.

Molecules in the food you eat

go inside the taste buds.

And nerves send taste messages

to your brain.

Then you taste your food.

Different parts of your tongue
pick up different tastes.
One part of your tongue
is best at tasting sweet things.
Another part is best at
tasting salty things.
Another part tastes sour things.
And still another part tastes
bitter things.

Try This

Test your tongue.

First find something sweet

—a piece of candy or gum.

Touch the <u>middle</u> of your tongue

with candy.

Do you taste a sweet taste?

Not very much.

Now touch the tip of your tongue.

You can taste the sweet taste much more!

That's because the tip

of your tongue has lots

of taste buds for sweet things.

Do the same thing with something sour,

something salty, and something bitter.

Make a map of your tongue.

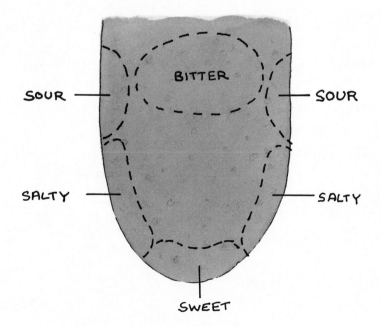

Your sense of taste gets

a lot of help

from your sense of smell.

Try This

Get two flavors of ice cream.

Ask a friend to close her eyes

and hold her nose.

Give her a taste of each flavor.

Can she tell which is which?

Probably not.

Then let your friend taste

the ice cream <u>without</u>

holding her nose.

It will be easy

to tell the flavors.

FEELING

You have nerves in your skin

for touch and pressure,

hot and cold, and pain.

Just by feeling, you can tell that

a pillow is soft,

a rock is hard,

a snowball is cold,

and a potato is hot.

The nerves in your skin tell your brain

all kinds of things.

Some parts of your body have more

touch nerves than others.

Try This

Ask a friend to close his eyes.

Spread two fingers apart.

Touch your friend quickly

on the palm of his hand.

Do it with both fingers at once.

Ask him, "How many fingers?"

Probably he will say, "Two."

Now touch your friend quickly

on his back.

Do it with the same two fingers.

How many does he feel?

Probably he will say, "One."

That's because there are many more

touch nerves on the palm

than on the back.

There are many other ways
to test your senses.
See if you can smell when
you're breathing <u>out</u>.
Or see bright light
with your eyes closed.

Or taste when you have a cold.

Does something feel smoother

when you rub it with your arm

or with your fingertips?

You can even try smelling a flower with your ear.

Good luck!